Volume 111 of the Yale Series of Younger Poets

Simulacra

Airea D. Matthews

FOREWORD BY CARL PHILLIPS

Yale UNIVERSITY PRESS

New Haven and London

Published with assistance from a grant to honor James Merrill.

Yale University Press books may be purchased in quantity for
educational, business, or promotional use. For information,
please e-mail sales.press@yale.edu (US office) or sales@
yaleup.co.uk (UK office).

Designed by Sonia Shannon.
Set in Fournier type by Integrated Publishing Solutions.
Printed in the United States of America.

Library of Congress Control Number: 2016952569
ISBN 978-0-300-22397-2 (hardcover : alk. paper)
ISBN 978-0-300-22396-5 (paperback : alk. paper)

A catalogue record for this book is available from the British
Library.

This paper meets the requirements of ANSI/NISO Z39.48-
1992 (Permanence of Paper).

10 9 8 7 6 5 4 3 2 1

for My Stalwart
and the Ghosts

What is a rebel? A man who says no, but whose refusal does not imply a renunciation.

—ALBERT CAMUS, *The Rebel: An Essay on Man in Revolt*

Contents

Foreword

Often, before actually settling into reading the poems of a manuscript, I'll look at how the poems present themselves on the page, their physical shape. When I put the poems of Airea D. Matthews's *Simulacra* to this test, an outright refusal of any formal conformity or predictability became immediately apparent. *Simulacra* offers us the poem as prose story, as an exchange of text messages with the dead, as collapsed opera, as Tweet, as letter, even as (in "If My Late Grandmother Were Gertrude Stein") a possible mash-up of rap, litany, and Stein's prosody circa *Tender Buttons*. The risk here is that the author may seem to lack formal control and/or restraint. In *Simulacra*, the use of wide-ranging form proves to be a deliberate prosodic strategy, a way of having the book as a whole enact the ceaseless hunger that is the book's thematic core.

The initial epigraph from Albert Camus points to rebellion, and indeed there's a kind of spine of rebellion that subtly governs *Simulacra*, inasmuch as the book opens with "Rebel Prelude," is roughly centered at "Rebel Opera," and ends with "Rebel Fugue." What is rebellion if not hunger for some form of change to the status quo? Early on, though, Matthews directs us to hunger that's more bodily, whose source is the mouth, an image that recurs frequently. Only two poems into the book, here is the fablelike "The Mine Owner's Wife":

> The bone china had been laid out. The napkins, threadbare,
> antiqued, yellowing. One gold-rimmed plate with butter in the
> trench. The wife asked, "How was your day?" His coal-mine
> mouthshaft widened, to make an utterance, managed only soot and
> one canary. Canary's wings, blackened and broken, tangled in the
> web above their heads, suspended in the chandelier's pendalogue.
> A spider eyed dinner, sharpened its knifeclaw. The mine owner
> dragged his fork's sharpened tine against his lip, rent his tongue. He
> bled all over the napkin, made pink the butter dish. His wife handed
> him her crystal goblet. He wrung his tongue over her glass, spilled
> garnet into her bowl. Filled his flute. They toasted.
> And, this, every single night.

Here, the mouth simultaneously becomes a mineshaft and the place of language, source both of financial livelihood and of utterance. The source, as well, though—from what I can tell—of the blood with which the couple's glasses are filled, before a toast that marks a thirst that, in turn, is at worst unslakable (given how this happens every night), at best ritualized. So the mouth, besides being the vehicle through which sustenance takes place, is as well the potential source of sustenance, but note how, in this poem at least, the price of sustenance is harm or damage, a slighter form of self-destruction.

No wonder, then, that Narcissus occurs so often in *Simulacra*—he whose desire for his own image, once Narcissus understood that it could never be consummated, led to his own death—by suicide, according to Ovid. The Narcissus image extends hunger beyond the body to the realm of emotion and psychology. And it is this kind of hunger—sheer want—with which Matthews seems most concerned, want and its often concomitant risks, not least the risk of losing a sense of self. From "On Meeting Want for the First Time":

> Smug bitch. Acted like I didn't exist.
> (What if she was right?)
> Tapped her shoulder, *Don't act like you don't see me!*
> She held her lips taut, as if threaded by fish wire, her gaze settled on
>   something behind me, *I see through you.*
>
> *Good. You see me, then?*
>
> *Nothing to see. Not much to your kind.*
>
> *Wait . . . who is my kind?*

Matthews suggests that yet another problem with want is that we see it as a means of confirmation that the self exists. If she passes us by, are we invisible? More troublingly, if we exist only within the context of desire, and if desire is linked as if inextricably to damage, what hope for us?

"Wait . . . who is my kind?" The resonance of that line with Anne Sexton's refrain (in "Her Kind") of "I have been her kind" hardly seems an accident, given how Anne Sexton appears on seven occasions in *Simulacra*.

In five instances, she is the Sexton we know of, the distinguished twentieth-century poet whose poems—and life, for that matter—famously meditated on and enacted a range of hungers: spiritual, sexual, and that no small, career-related hunger that at best (and truest, maybe) is a steady ambition for the art itself. Weirdly, but somehow believably despite anachronism, in these five instances Sexton is involved in a text exchange (the pun of Sexton on sexting as a form of texting does not go unnoticed, likewise the double meaning of the word "text" itself) with, variously, a dead addict's daughter, a backslider, Quiet Desperation, an ingenue, and Tituba (she of the Salem witch trials). Hunger seems largely the subject of these texts that have a deliberate drifting quality, a disembodiedness that seems consistent enough with the medium of texting, but also seems as good a way as any of getting at the ultimate impossibility of plumbing the nature of want:

why burn, why
make matters worse
squandering impulse?
who needs want?

("An Ingenue Texts Sexton before the Honey Moon")

It's an impossibility matched apparently by the impossibility of escaping want, since Sexton often seems no freer of desire in death:

My fingers still smell like
last night's spent seed.

I wonder if he
has washed me off.
Watercolor,
Watercolor

("Quiet Desperation Texts Sexton on Independence Day")

the last three lines, of course, an allusion to the end of Sexton's poem "For
My Lover, Returning to His Wife." In these text poems, Sexton functions
as a slippery Sibyl figure; she is viewed as a source of answers, though
her answers are decidedly slant, more like responses that may or may not
connect with the questions, the largest of which continues, again even in
death, to be herself.

Matthews presents us with Sexton two additional times; in these, how-
ever, Sexton is a nurse who attends a speaker recovering from addiction at
a rehabilitation center:

I know how I got here, and yet
I have no idea how I got here.
The sole respite offered by a nurse-raven, who pulls me from
that wreckage for routine vital checks. Her name is Anne Sexton.
I told Anne a famous poet had her name, but was no longer
alive—death by asphyxiation, suicide. Anne Sexton promises
she'll read Anne Sexton one day, then asks how I'm doing.
Never been better, Anne. Never better.

("Meeting Anne Sexton")

So many questions arise from this scene. What does it mean, to have made a name for oneself as a poet, if others don't know you existed? What, if anything, do the hungers that drove the art even as they destroyed the maker amount to in the end? Is it enough to be the nurse Anne Sexton without any knowledge of the poet? Who is Anne Sexton? What, finally, is a self at all?

I've gone on at some length here about Sexton, because the use of the poet Sexton as a character/speaker seems one way for Matthews to sustain a meditation on yet another dominant theme of the book, that of addiction. And somewhere also lies the notion of legacy. In Sexton's case, literary legacy is the point, but for Matthews the concern is with the relation between addiction and familial legacy. I mentioned a dead drug addict's daughter earlier. Another daughter of an addict appears in "Rebel Opera," in a scene that occurs entirely in a father's mouth: his daughter, wife, and an oboe player are sitting in the father's mouth, having a conversation. The daughter longs to break free, but her mother counters with:

We inherit the cause, not the illness.
. . . .
Want moves between or up
or down or through the bloodline.
Desire is spacious.
Want's in the DNA.

It's an answer the daughter refuses in words but seems by her actions to confirm:

I can't . . . I won't . . . I've got to break free from this low-rent
    bullshit . . .
(hums as she grinds a pill to snortdust with a platinum card)
                    (Father swallows)
                    Fade to Black

One constructible narrative for *Simulacra* is that of a recovering addict—herself the daughter of an addict—reflecting on the seeming inescapability of addiction. The particular thrill of *Simulacra* is Matthews's resistance to an easy confessional mode; instead, she offers us nothing less than an extended meditation on the multifariousness of desire; addiction is only one manifestation of it, and hardly, she suggests, the worst one.

I mentioned the mouth as the source of language and its utterance. Isn't language itself a form of desire, an *attempt* at pinning the too-often-inexplicable down, an attempt because language proves to be an unreliable medium? And yet if language is our chief way of communicating, what are the consequences for any human interaction? Or as Matthews puts it at one point:

When I anatomically re-construct your absence and step inside
nothing, intoning "i.you.i.you.us.we.," how am I to know pronouns
translate to *war* in your language?

                    ("The Lover Problem in Analogue
                    [from Wittgenstein's *Lost Black Book*]")

Meanwhile, of whatever gets said with language, how to distinguish between truth and lies, the mouth again as the source of both? Matthews makes frequent reference to the twentieth-century philosopher and theorist Jean Baudrillard, most immediately in her title: *Simulacra* is the book in which Baudrillard insists, among other things, that there *is* no truth. There's only that which hides the truth's nonexistence; and by that action, as I understand it, it becomes the truth or maybe a stand-in for truth—a cover, really, for how there's nothing, by pretending to be something. But if there is no truth, is everything a lie? At the very least, this line of thinking leads to moral vagueness; if nothing is fixed, in terms of how to behave, where does that leave us with regard to the various desires and addictions we've been wrestling with? Why wrestle?

One reason might be in order to know oneself better. Surely the positions we stake out for ourselves with respect to whatever moral constructs arise say something about who we are, about the moral compass we fashion for ourselves as guide, however shifting. But if there is no truth, there is no morality, nothing to distinguish correct versus incorrect behavior. Meanwhile, we also largely come to know ourselves in the context of others, via language. Back to unreliability—especially, Matthews seems to say, in a time where communication itself has been reduced to the quick surfaces, abbreviations, and emojis of social media. In a sense, everything stays alive in the era of the internet—nothing's entirely lost, including, apparently, Anne Sexton, alive and texting. But even the distinction between life and death seems at risk, based on the texts of Tituba that conclude "Sexton Texts Tituba from a Bird Conservatory":

FRI., JULY 2, 10:29 PM
LOL! But I'm not dead, huh?

FRI., JULY 2, 11:21 PM
I'm not dead, right?

SAT., JULY 3, 3:00 AM
Anne? I'm not, right?

∎

It will be I? It will be the silence, where I am? I don't know, I'll
never know: in the silence you don't know.

You must go on.

I can't go on.

I'll go on.

So ends Samuel Beckett's *The Unnameable*, a novel with which Matthews is
surely familiar. Matthews has conjured in *Simulacra* a twenty-first-century re-
visiting, extending, and reinventing of Beckett's idea of existence as relentless
existential crisis. She does the most honest thing a poet can do: she presents
us with the conundrum of being alive and human without pretending to have
the power to unriddle it. "The fiercest / warriors know when to turn their
backs" ("Sekhmet After Hours"), says Sekhmet, the ancient Egyptian warrior-
goddess who strikes me as one of Matthews's alter egos. In this poem, one of

her three appearances in *Simulacra*, Sekhmet has taken off her lion head for the evening: "The lion's head roars, side eyes my image / hoping not to face another of our undoings." That reference to undoing suggests that even warriors are vulnerable; to what, though? Here's all of "Sekhmet's Query":

> Though isn't it true, at some point,
> assuming no air resistance, a stone
> thrown upward with great velocity
> will escape humble gravity?

I see this question—as I see inquiry itself—as a manifestation of hope: we ask, because we believe in answers, and hope to attain them. And yet to hope is to be vulnerable, to the possibility at the very least of finding no answer, or not the one we hoped for. "Sekhmet's Query" comes very near *Simulacra*'s end, and seems Matthews's way of telling us that without hope, even in the context of moral ambiguity, we are surely lost. The poems of *Simulacra* offer none of the falseness of consolation but instead provoke us to consider that our best hope, ultimately, might be to

> surrender to the notes in our pulse

> exhaust both pain and pleasure

> until, winded, we come up
> for air

("Rebel Fugue")

CARL PHILLIPS

SIMULACRA

Everywhere we live in a universe strangely similar to the original—
things are doubled by their own scenario.

—JEAN BAUDRILLARD, *Simulacra and Simulation*

MEETING WANT

This is where seduction begins.

—JEAN BAUDRILLARD, *Simulacra and Simulation*

REBEL PRELUDE

in the garden
or our bedroom, we'd made love or

fought about bushes—
hydrangea or rhododendron

purple ivies climbing our back fence,
opal basil wilting, one of us

had forgotten to water her or was it
autumn and she was dying on her own?

either way, the infested pepper dangling by
frayed browning stem threads caught

our attention—*how did that parasite get inside?*—
you mumbled about larvae.

but I knew it was a winged thing,
a puncture, a black and wicked door.

THE MINE OWNER'S WIFE

The bone china had been laid out. The napkins, threadbare, antiqued, yellowing. One gold-rimmed plate with butter in the trench. The wife asked, "How was your day?" His coal-mine mouthshaft widened, to make an utterance, managed only soot and one canary. Canary's wings, blackened and broken, tangled in the web above their heads, suspended in the chandelier's pendalogue. A spider eyed dinner, sharpened its knifeclaw. The mine owner dragged his fork's sharpened tine against his lip, rent his tongue. He bled all over the napkin, made pink the butter dish. His wife handed him her crystal goblet. He wrung his tongue over her glass, spilled garnet into her bowl. Filled his flute. They toasted.

And, this, every single night.

LETTERS TO MY WOULD-BE LOVER ON GEOMETRY AND PONDS

Dear _____,

Mostly all of them come true. In one dream, a handful of crumbs cast on Lethe—instead of slow float—engulfed by fire. When I awoke, sweat-drenched, she asked if I liked rivers and if I wanted toast for breakfast since the bacon cooked down to sticks.

Dear _____,

When has blood ever stopped men? Why would it?

Dear _____,

I don't know when I knew. Was it after she drank me the first time, or the nights that followed? Who is to say? I do know I came to fully under-stand Narcissus. Imagine sitting by that pond only to find you are the water and you were very, very thirsty.

Dear _____,

The worst geometry: circles. Unanimated, flat, predictable—and if you ask me—Ouroboros is one sorry, spun-out, tail-in-his-mouth son-of-a-bitch.

Dear _____,

I meant to tell the truth, over and over. But each time I opened my mouth, echoes: *I'll be home late, again. Late again? What did you say? You don't say? Beloved, how was your day? And your day?*

Dear _____,

It wasn't easy for her either, in love with two women: a gorgon and a siren. The siren would plead: *Crash at this rock!* The gorgon would stare her still. Wave or stone, skipped water pebble. Hard choices.

Dear _____,

Nights alone. I would sweetly sing the sailors' song in the mirror, hoping to force myself into some sea. Hush the whirling gusts of please.

TEMPTATION OF THE COMPOSER

Oh Shepherd, our honeyed marriage
      bed in the meadow was too narrow
and though you herd wild things,
      you were deaf to my footsteps.
As you lay there in the dew of me, curled,
      satiated, I tiptoed backwards
toward our door under twisted reeds.

      Out where pasture led to brackish
waters and red-hot mists rose from quartz
      I lowered myself into rockpores
while rushing wings of screech owls
      seemed to sing: *Welcome, Dark-Light*

              Welcome, Wild-Love

Home

      Home

            Away

HERO(i)N

i thought it was a bird. skimmed rush. hush as before a fowl fixes

    its head up from shadow water

sickened by its own nature, narcissus-

               reversed. unfortunate predatory

consequence. the luck. heron spots two ducklings nesting on an outcrop

    of rocks.

swift-like. heron bounces off the lake, a hollowed pebble. in one swallow

    babes go

down. pulsing inside heron's throat until they succumb. mama

       mallard squawks and plods—helpless, she flies low

away. how long do mother ducks mourn—until the next day

       next month, until pitch pines

shake barren

    or a naked beggar shakes on his kitchen floor like

breccia in a rain stick, begging: *2 bird bags, 4 quarters, 1 gram?* his

daughters

      empty cupboards, offer open tin at his feet—*eat, eat*—until

         heron comes. when sick,

fowl fit in veins like ducks in necks—vortex of sorts.

                some knew this.

         yet, none bothered to explain how

heron

made him fly

         why heron

                made him

well, less starved.

Smug bitch. Acted like I didn't exist.

(What if she was right?)

Tapped her shoulder, *Don't act like you don't see me!*

She held her lips taut, as if threaded by fish wire, her gaze settled on something

behind me, *I see through you.*

    Good. You see me, then?

Nothing to see. Not much to your kind.

    Wait . . . who is my kind?

*See-through. Peek-a-boo. Wanter who wants and doesn't know why. Knower
who knows and doesn't know what. She who is and doesn't know who. Mesh
veil. Ordinary invisible.*

THE GOOD DENTIST'S WIFE

By their platinum anniversary, the missus' incisors floated in a water-filled Ball jar on the kitchen windowsill. Her cuspids in a satin pouch in the first drawer of the nightstand, near his side. Her bicuspids buried with the azaleas. Molars were everywhere, some ground to dust. They made a deliciously light breading for the stuffed zucchini, a family favorite.

The year of their paper anniversary he almost strayed, because Ms. Pomona needed an extraction. Pomona with every fruit wanting to be plucked, right there, right in his office and the question of men's strength. But the good dentist went home and told his wife how the pulling awakened some urge in him, an arousal as Pomona's full breasts heaved just below his forearm. After confessing, he sat alone, whimpering. That good dentist's wife, empathetic and young, wanted to give her husband what he needed. She told him to take one of her teeth. She had so many, then.

Now when the earth revolves, on the same date, she readies and he takes. Afterward, he thrusts his tongue in her mouth, massages the bald ridge where her crown was, where the root hid—renewing their vows in a covenant of bloodlust and sacrifice.

Why just the other day, at the local diner, after their 32nd ritual,
he remarked on his blushing bride's beauty. The waitress appeared
bewildered, not seeing what he saw. But the missus giggled in her palm,
covered her mouth with her hands. All the while, the good dentist eyed
the waitress' full, gap-toothed smile, his familiar longing surfaced.

MEETING ANNE SEXTON

If you're lucky the constant mask will get you this:
one stalwart lover who fills out your paperwork when you can't
remember your name, a beige room with one 6-foot table, a chorus
of moans and whistles from the girl next door who smiles misery
for 5 hours, adults arguing over who kicked in the most walls, an alien
who sucks her thumb to still her hands and avoids humans because
of their nervous eyes, the manchild who writes his name in all caps
on the top of a perpetually empty Styrofoam cup, a jaundiced new mother
who lifts up her shirt to play drums on her stretch-marked belly—
she knows only one song, AC/DC's "For Those about to Rock"—,
an elderly brother from the deep South who speaks Gullah—but not
to you, about you to everyone else—"uh tell'er say dat gal geechee,"
a chain-smoking, Jesus-freak therapist with questionable credentials
who believes salvation is the cure for every ailment known to man
—including bat-shit crazy—
and the suburban pill-popping housewife who needs to know
if she can touch my hair—*are they braids or weave?*—and
if I can do her hair—*I wish I had kinks too!*—and if
we can be best friends forever after this tornadic hell is behind

the both of us. We huddle daily around the 6-foot table and commit
to staging elaborate rebellions, deploying pharmico allies to flank
the shadows of old wounds. I am silent, or numb.
I know how I got here, and yet
I have no idea how I got here.
The sole respite offered by a nurse-raven, who pulls me from
that wreckage for routine vital checks. Her name is Anne Sexton.
I told Anne a famous poet had her name, but was no longer
alive—death by asphyxiation, suicide. Anne Sexton promises
she'll read Anne Sexton one day, then asks how I'm doing.
Never been better, Anne. Never better.

. . . AND REPEATING

You can't fight the code . . . can we fight DNA?

—JEAN BAUDRILLARD, *Symbolic Exchange and Death*

SEXTON TEXTS A DEAD ADDICT'S DAUGHTER DURING POLAR VORTEX

THURS., JAN. 19, 3:18 PM
"Let us eat air, rock, coal, iron.
Turn, my hungers."

THURS., JAN. 19, 3:21 PM
Meanwhile, I'm trying. God knows.

THURS., JAN. 19, 4:01 PM
But mother unearthed each small
bloodmain under her gauzed wrists.
She fought a strange compulsion
to press her mouth against her
right pulse, taste the throbbing
veiny eels her crooked lovers forsook
drink from blind lakes of their leaving,
undo their digging.

THURS., JAN. 19, 4:32 PM
Sharp brick ledge,
deep scarp fault,
no matter how much silt
I packed into the hole,
no matter . . .

THURS., JAN. 19, 4:33 PM
Trenches never fill.

THURS., JAN. 19, 4:38 PM
never could unslope
else I'd cease being
sorry's shallow shelter.

SAT., JAN. 21, 7:17 AM
Ice storms, splintering
crystals, of course. Today,
everything wheels and bone
strike, every slick black
lies under rock
salt.

SAT., JAN. 21, 8:01 AM
(1/5) Every day, my father fell six
feet into a vat of tar. Burned
his neck, ankles, veins. We
saw his viscous shoeprints
blanched blisters and salve.
Hours after, when
he touched any door
knob, steam rose
from the brass.

SAT., JAN. 21, 8:03 AM
(3/5) Recall he wanted
to go home, meaning,
maybe,

SAT., JAN. 21, 8:02 AM
(2/5) He died for the last time
on a Monday, or Tuesday or
Wednesday or was it Thursday or
Friday?

SAT., JAN. 21, 8:06 AM
(5/5) point is: he died
at some point
during some week

SAT., JAN. 21, 8:05 AM
(4/5) back to tar streets

MEETING WANT (AGAIN)

Empty street. No lampposts. No buildings. No pavement. We spin inside a tornado funnel.

Dizzy, I yelled, *Want, I never asked for you.*

She spoke barely above a whisper yet, somehow, her breath broke through the fevered whip, *Jaded Ingenue. It's not in your words but your body. Where's your head, anyway?*

I shouted—*On my nightstand with my other faces*—adjusted my belted dress, stuffed my breasts inside my bra cup, tossed my hair to the left, reapplied MAC Ready-the-Red lipstick and turned away.

Want laughed. Her voice to my back, *See you soon, sooner than soon.*

I walked out of the twisting into a familiar vacancy, inside a man's mouth, wave of his tongue. I swung from his uvula. My mother, smoking a Newport nearby, instructed, *Say hello to your father, Dear.* Snuffed out her cig on his bottom lip, *Now, what are you doing with your hair these days?*

AN INGENUE TEXTS SEXTON BEFORE
THE HONEY MOON

time presses me.
why burn, why
make matters worse
squandering impulse?
who needs want?

I close garden gates,
pinch back my shoots,
feed hungers to
the meadows of sounds,
lie down flat on thorns.
There,

daydream the first bedding out
boxspring, dappled sleep,
woodscrape, moon singe
numb us both

where juniper needs pruning,
prick, pull in drenched.
Only Gaia knows what blooming
comes & she grows silent.

MON., APR. 13, 5:33 PM
like waning dragonflies
sprawled and spent on gravel
purged of fire.

MON., APR. 13, 5:39 PM
The irony, of course:
how dragonflies cast
their frigid bodies
during summer
called to winter
before autumn arrives.

FROM THE POCKET OF HIS LIP

S moke rose under my father's tongue. There, a strange man with
an oboe sat on the ridge of his tooth, playing wide vibratos
through nimbusfog. I asked why he was there, too.

Fine-tuning the orchestra of lies.

I nodded. They play beautifully, don't they?

Especially in your key. Hum for me.

SEXTON TEXTS A BACKSLIDER AFTER BREAKING LENT

WED., FEB. 11, 10:01 PM
My hunger . . . my stomach
makes me suffer.

WED., FEB. 11, 10:05 PM
Anne, Sister, flee on your donkey.

WED., FEB. 11, 11:59 PM
But he was my savior, my husband;
look how I made his suffering
worse than scourge of crucifixion.

THURS., FEB. 12, 12:01 AM
Jesus hung for only one
sun-rust afternoon.

THURS., FEB. 12, 12:10 AM
How many years was I married?
How many stripes, thorns, crosses?

THURS., FEB. 12, 12:11 AM
Thieves choke out
on the sacroplank.
What you think killed God?

THURS., FEB. 12, 12:23 AM
God slew himself—
willed thirst—
anemic vow soaked

in gall and vinegar,
save what can't be
salvaged.

Imagine three days of God
gone missing. Now,
imagine my lifetime of it.

Better to build
your own sepulcher
inside an idling Charger—
gorged and crimson.

I'd rather roll up on God's
pearly in a blood-red
Benz or BMW.

Any fancy casket will do.

REBEL OPERA

(The opening scene begins inside the father's mouth. Mother and Daughter resting on the pillow of his bottom lip after daily brushing and flossing his one remaining tooth.)

ACT I

DAUGHTER:

How do we get the fuck out of here?

MOTHER:

That's not discussed, Dear.

No one has ever tried.

And watch your mouth!

OBOIST:

(sounds the note)

ORCHESTRA:

(tunes to standard pitch)

DAUGHTER:

But what do we eat?

MOTHER:

We eat whatever he eats.

We eat whatever we catch.

DAUGHTER:

(clutches her growling stomach)

I'm starving.

MOTHER:

So is he.

We all are, especially those outside.

They'll consume anything out there.

Safer here.

(catches a wren that flies in his mouth)

OBOIST:

(sets the key in C minor)

ORCHESTRA:

(plays Schubert's "Wanderer Fantasy")

DAUGHTER:

I can't stay inside. I'm claustrophobic. I'm . . .

(paces and tries to distract herself with erratic movement)

MOTHER:

No exceptions.

He's sick, you know? The virus . . .

(brushes her hair)

DAUGHTER:

That virus? The one carried in fluids?

We'll get it, too! Haven't you noticed the rains?

(opens her umbrella)

MOTHER:

It doesn't work like that.

We inherit the cause, not the illness.

DAUGHTER:

Drugs? Needles? Blood?

(drops umbrella and thumbs through her wallet for a loose white pill)

MOTHER:

Jaws without hinges.

Want moves between or up

or down or through the bloodline.

Desire is spacious.

Want's in the DNA.

OBOIST:

(nods)

ORCHESTRA:

(increases tempo)

DAUGHTER:

I can't . . . I won't . . . I've got to break free from this low-rent bullshit . . .

(hums as she grinds a pill to snortdust with a platinum card)

FATHER:

(swallows)

Fade to Black

PIOUS

In dreams, Mary comes draped beneath a veil, Dead
Sea breaking at her feet, arms outstretched in that maternal
welcoming. She wades waist deep, covers her scars, not
wanting to scare the children. Every mother's duty:
Keep the unholy origins hidden, those hauntings quiet.
Like her, I cloak my immaculates in robes, send them off
to learn. Soon they'll wonder, though, about the white
detritus on my tongue when they come home, as I nod off
mid-endearment, weighing hope against their smiles, our
heavy good nights before the tiny Mary in my well shakes
her bottle full of pills, beckoning:
Take, eat,
in remembrance—

    And who am I not to answer my own heritable call?

SEKHMET'S CONCEIT

—As if light were the remedy

for the pitch thrall of fate, I could

angle beams toward the desert,

stream across dark chasms of space,

reveal this enemy's backbone,

uncoil that helix . . .

WANT 1:1: In the beginning was pussy and it was good.[2] Now the earth was formless and barren inside her deep. The famished spirit of the Gods moved.[3] And they said, *Let there be moonshine*, and she made moonshine and separated her sustenance from their hunger.[4] They called her morning.[5] She misheard mourning.[6] Pussy wept. Sin entered.

∞

BITCH 66:6: Hera commanded Ganymede to do her dirty bidding. Ganymede begged her mercy, explaining: *But Zeus swooped down as a black eagle in plumes, dug his talons into my ankle and dragged me here.*[7] Hera countered: *You were born thirsting a mouthful of ichor from any God who would oblige. Suffering follows quench.*

∞

LONGING 4:2: Flesh is a constant haunting.[3] And since every womb conceives a haint, life starts an empty egg.

∞

PROPHETS 6:13: Penelope filled Odysseus' absence with other beastly bodies.[14] Her suitors took their fill, and Penelope begat Pan.[15] Later, Pan's fondness for bare breasts and vacant flasks? It is written, men seek their mothers anyplace they can.

∞

JEALOUS 5:1: Nymphs were much lower than goddesses. They were nubile and beautiful; youthful, yes, but without choice.[2] Nymphs took what they could get.[3] Nymphs never confronted the goddess' conundrum:

To fuck Heracles or slay some beast or bed Orpheus and be lulled to sleep or none or all.

∞

CHAOS 30:7: Darkness was here first.[8] Light is a gentrifier. Darkness is not called un-light. Light is un-dark.

LETTERS TO MY WOULD-BE LOVER ON DOLLS AND REPEATING

Dear _____,

Girl Scout for 2 years, then I quit. I can tie 37 types of knots. I can untie none of them.

Dear _____,

I don't understand when you wrote, "I am full of shit, imbalanced and you can't stand me." I don't want to be presumptuous, so I'll just wait to hear back. I have a tendency to read into things.

Dear _____,

Things are a language. I once read that in a horribly written book. When mother neglected me, she'd buy me a doll. I hated dolls. Yet, there was something oddly comforting in getting the thing I didn't want.
I'd opt for a Barbie, of course. I'd get home and pile her into her pink Barbie Dream House with the others. I didn't even bother prying the box tethers off her neck. I liked them. They reminded me of a noose.

Dear _____,

A faith healer/psychic/medium/pagan/evangelist told me I could raise dead things. I don't actually know what that means. Seems selfish to rouse someone from eternal slumber because I'm sleepwalking.

Dear _____,

I never asked your name. May I call you Lazarus?

Dear _____,

Eleven. Lost it to a Ken doll. Don't tell anyone. It was one of those secrets shared between childhood friends. Whenever she slept over, we would take our hard Kens and rub their smooth plastic heads against our pussies. I could hear her moan. I feigned sighing. My fingers knew me better. I needed something more from Ken. I took him into me, up to the shoulders. When I pulled him out, blood from his head dripped down his torso. Ken had that same picket-tooth smile, pinkish though, none the worse for wear. And I swear I felt him breathing.

Dear _____,

Not much to tell. I stockpiled that one with all the Barbies. Once I had him he was no use to me anymore.

Dear _____,

Same as yours. Father was a moody bastard genius. And I don't know if I blame drugs or schizophrenia. I do know I worry. Lunacy is genetic, I'm told.

Anyway, I'm off to pick up some shiraz and my prescriptions. Nothing serious: one to stay awake, one to fall asleep, one to feel normal, one to feel.

BLIND CALCULUS (FROM BARTHES'
A LOVER'S DISCORD)

> In the amorous realm, the most painful wounds are inflicted more
> often by what one sees than by what one knows.
> —ROLAND BARTHES, *The Lover's Discourse*

Well past midday, mottled sunlight through ice fractals. It's the logged-in name and password. Careful codes in which he means you, they means he and she (ß) divided by it (Ω) plus her $\neq$ μ plus $\sqrt{}$ of who else $\pm$ pronouns plus nickel (Ni) plus gold (Au) minus sum (Σ) plus silence minus Δ plus inquiry minus π multiplied by one = pattern $\approx$ 0, where 0 means there is no one in the one's place or any other place in the placeholder. If there are numbers other than 0 in the other placeholders, this complicated equation is best represented by the lemniscate (∞).

QUIET DESPERATION TEXTS SEXTON ON INDEPENDENCE DAY

(1/2) Because there was no other place
I went home
back before dawn
away from the scene of crazy-making,
heightened senses.

SAT., JULY 3, 8:15 AM
(2/2) my purse wide, thighs wet
keys set down
bedroom bound
where the baby also sleeps.
Tiptoed like a strange thief.
Thought of my blotted-out x's—
this is the mind's prison
not a game
not a playground.

SAT., JULY 3, 10:31 AM
Sorry. Fell asleep reading Rimbaud.
Same dress from last night.
Once I would have thought nothing
of this. Today I feel like Gomer before
Hosea chose her. Maybe I will conjure

Jezebel or Tamar through the oracle.
They were thrown into
Hell, too.

I'm hardly ever alone
but when children wander
the day gifts me time to
recall that same dream:
dead deer mice in the garage,
albino possums, unlocked doors.

If I draw my blinds tightly
enough sunlight loiters
smoky dust begs to be let in
like a Maine Coon on Sunset,
outside double panes,
in the throes of heat.

Morning. Ants run errands.
My kitchen floor finds them
second-line marching to crumbs
tri-sected bodies shouldering
trash twice their size,
all that wasted strength!

(2/2) Such Titans,
Atlas, sky vaulters!
I made that up,
but do you get it?

SUN., JULY 4, 7:51 AM
(1/2) Dumb-muscled foragers
pack meal lumps
fallen from some child's
grubby hands, not even for themselves.
Long live the queen! Nobles eat
well & often. Social orders exist
in every world on every back.

THURS., AUG. 1, 10:49 AM
(2/2) Her son rides up and down
my dead end to drown out
his mother's yell. He nods to me.
I sign for a package . . .

THURS., AUG. 1, 11:01 AM
My fingers still smell like
last night's spent seed.
I wonder if he
has washed me off.
Watercolor,
Watercolor

THURS., AUG. 1, 10:47 AM
(1/2) distant, muffled droning,
one neighbor lives in his shed
saws wood all day for a project
he can't afford to finish.
Outside, the Jamaican lady
screams to her estranged lover,

"I don't know ya'! Ya' come to
m'door ev'ryday beggin'."

FRI., AUG. 2, 12:01 AM
A lifetime of such small reminders
A lifetime of blotted outs coming
on or in. This fucking hunger!
This fucking!

FRI., AUG. 2, 12:07 AM
Should have common-lawed
a white boy, moved to Amsterdam,
had mixed-up, nappy-headed babies.

FRI., AUG. 2, 12:15 AM
Strangers would call you "mammy"
for taking your tiny joys public.
This is the small life with long days in it
& nothing to force clock hands closer

FRI., AUG. 2, 6:41 AM
(2/2) around the block.
Fewer asses not tweaked,
twerked or fatted, yet
all that holds back a soul?
Chalkcage withering under
wrinkled corsets

FRI., AUG. 2, 6:39 AM
Every here
same cawing crows,
same ruined perches.

(1/2) Same old hoes in fresh loam
and the bald cuckold who drags
his tucked wife's fat dog
while he jogs

THE LOVER PROBLEM IN ANALOGUE (FROM WITTGENSTEIN'S *LOST BLACK BOOK*)

If I give someone the order *fetch me the black flower from the florist*, is he to know what sort of dahlias to bring, as I have only given him a string of *words*?

If you want her to see your sky and she asks which sky is *yours* while you point to Hydra, how is she to know sky is not a constellation of chthonic monsters?

When I anatomically re-construct your absence and step inside nothing, intoning "i.you.i.you.us.we.," how am I to know pronouns translate to *war* in your language?

I left our window open most nights. A man with winged ankles would visit while you slept. He'd ask about my doings, how the Syrah finished, noticed the dimple on my chin when I smiled, touched the thick swell of my waist, lightly. When the wind whistled like the Northeast Corridor, he'd tongue the small of my back before leaving. After 2 most mornings. I wailed a tempest that last time. Flooded our basement. Asked him to stay or carry me over. He tucked me in the crook of his elbow and flew here. Where I am now.

When you woke the next morning, I imagine you thought it rained the night before. You called the plumber, didn't you? To fix the basement, swollen from squalls? Did you dig your fingernail under the blistering cinder? Check for mold? Did the walls crumble? When you asked the children where their mother was, did they shrug? Bounce my name between rooms? Weep into their porridge? If they beat their bare feet against the cracked tiles in the hallway, did you notice those tiny feathers sprouting from their Achilles' heels? Did you wrinkle your brow? Grab your shears?

DODECAPHONY

"regard all present universe, the effects
from past which cause its future."

regard effects which the past universe present—its future from cause—all
regard past universe which effects cause, it's all present from future, the
past all present from the effects cause future universe which (some) regard.

"and that future like distant past would
remain present, opening our eyes."

present future that like past distant would remain opening and our eyes
past, distant, would remain and our eyes opening that future like present
opening and our future eyes that present like distant past would remain.

CAN? (FROM WITTGENSTEIN'S *LOST BLACK BOOK*)

Explain the word "can."
Can a machine be lonely? Man as cog-lightning widget. Vast industrial
tiny. Glossed conveyor-belt enabler.

Day laborers may argue "machines can't be other than machines."

But, what are the hours of day laborers?

What if lonely happens at night?
Keen blooms. We only ever know what we've seen.

I'll say no more about this now.

Can you run your nimble finger down a myth's spinethread at 3 am?
How do you know?

WHO.

One should distrust the humility of mirrors.

—Jean Baudrillard, *Seduction*

IF MY LATE GRANDMOTHER WERE
GERTRUDE STEIN

I. SOUTHERN MIGRATION

Leech. Broke speech. Leaf ain't pruning pot. Lay. Lye. Lie. Hair straight
off. Arrowed branch and horse joint. Elbow ash. Row fish. Row dog. Slow-
milk pig. Blue-water sister. Hogs like willow. Weep crow. Weep cow. Sow
bug. Soul narrow. Inchway. Inches away. Over the bridge. Back that way.
Fur. Fir needles in coal. Black hole. Black out. Black feet. Blame. Long
way still.   Not there.   There. Here.   Same.

II. FEED THE SAW

Old Crow. Liquor. Drink. Drunk. Girdle. Grits. Grit. Tea. Grit tea.
Tea git. Get shaved. Shook. Shucked. Shit. Flour. Flower. Lard and
swallow. Hardedge chew. Chipped tooth bite. Tool chip. Bite. Bloat.
Bloat. Bloat. Blight seat. Blight sit tea. Be light city. Down town
dim. Slight dark. Old Arc. New Arc. New Ark. New work. Newark.
Lark-fed. Corned bread. Bedfeather back. Sunday-shack church fat.
Greased-gloved. Dust-rubbed. Cheap-heeled shoe. Window seat.
Mirror eye. Window. I. Window. Window. When though. When
though. Wind blow. November. December. No cinder. No slumber.

No summer. Branch. Branched. Blanched. Fried. Freed. Fly.   Want.
What.   Want. What. Graves want.

III. MISCEGENATION

Good. Smooth. Curly haired baby. Baby rock-a-bye. My baby. Mama
rock-a-bye that baby. Wrestle the earth, baby. No dirt. No. Dirt-shine.
Shine. Shine-neck. Porcelain. Tin. Tarnish. Powder milk. Pout her.
Milk. Powder-silk inheritance. Front the washtub. Top the bed. Bin.
Leaky numbers run in. Run in. Run on. Red fevers hold your palm.
Sweat it out. Hot. Hot. Heat the rest. Pretty melt that wax. Wide flower.
Ellis-Island daddy. O, Daddy's bar. Banned. Mongrel hum. Come.
Come now. Little bones bend. Old crack. Creak. Crank. Crick. Curly
Q. Fuck. Them. Then fuck them. You hear me. Walk through
good-haired baby. Half   of you.   Belong.

IV. GERTRUDE STEIN

Who. Bills mount. Picasso. Who. Matisse. Who. Mortgage. No currency
canvass. Pay brushes. Stroke. Stroke. Bridge. Brittle. Blend. 10 miles
daybreak. 10 miles they break. We broke. No brick. Widgets in the
envelope. No railroad green. Agriculture. Pea snap. Earth under nails.
Spine and stilt woman. Roach-kill heel woman. Roaches in the crawl.
Woman, creep. Keep 5th grade. Every where. Wear every where. We're

every. Where. Any. How. We sacrifice and hammer. They sacrifice the hammer. Never. Ax and hatchet make callous. Hard hand. Prison-pen privilege. Prison. Privilege pinned. Bar-thorn pinned. Pine cross. Crown. Weight. Weight. Wait. Iron is harder. Chicken fat can is full of spark. Spark kill. Ore. Sparkle. Or. Spark cull. Spark. Cull. Hoe. Heave-ho. Heave-holy. Heavy. Heavy. Heavy lights genius. That is that Gertrude. Who.

DESCENT OF THE COMPOSER

When I mention the ravages of now, I mean to say, then.
I mean to say the rough-hewn edges of time and space,
a continuum that folds back on itself in furtive attempts
to witness what was, what is, and what will be. But what

I actually mean is that time and space have rough-hewn edges.
Do I know this for sure? No, I'm no astrophysicist. I have yet
to witness what was, what is, and what will be. But what
I do know, I know well: bodies defying spatial constraint.

Do I know this for sure? No, I'm no scientist. I have yet
to prove that defiant bodies even exist as a theory; I offer
what I know. I know damn well my body craves the past tense,
a planet in chronic retrograde, searching for sun's shadow.

As proof that defiant bodies exist in theory, I even offer
what key evidence I have: my life and Mercury's swift orbits, or
two planets in chronic retrograde, searching for sun's shadow—
which is to say—two objects willfully disappearing from present view.

Perhaps life is nothing more than swift solar orbits, or dual
folds along a continuum that collapse the end and the beginning,
which implies people can move in reverse, will their own vanishing;
or at least relive the ravages of then—right here, right now.

SEXTON TEXTS TITUBA FROM A BIRD CONSERVATORY

—for Margaret Walker and Molly Means

FRI., JULY 2, 7:07 PM
"Eat, the stones a poor man breaks,"

FRI., JULY 2, 7:18 PM
Still stale as they were
when Memaw died.
Half-mad on working-class
hunger; plumpness thinned
to a chip of lamb's bone,
legs decayed, necrotic.

FRI., JULY 2, 7:26 PM
Running is a game
for the young. Women
of a certain age, root.

FRI., JULY 2, 9:09 PM
Some rot gashing cane
with dull machetes. Sinking in
clay around 10-foot stalks when
all the while they could have been
coal-eyed peacocks, lean deep-water
ghosts, spunforce bladefeathers,
fear itself.

56 Who.

Can you believe I still carry
the knife my husband gave me?
I gut, hollow and scrape
soft spoil from cavities, but
what's dead is pretty well empty.

FRI., JULY 2, 9:21 PM
Good on you. Makes for easy work.
My people are steel-clad nomads
at the full-metal brink. None
know what's in the chamber,
staring down our barrels.

FRI., JULY 2, 9:32 PM
There's 2 ways to terrify men:
tell them what's coming,
don't tell them what's next . . .

FRI., JULY 2, 9:55 PM
(2/2) deathbed—herons,
black merlins, white-necked
ravens, mute cygnus, Impundulu—

FRI., JULY 2, 9:54 PM
(1/2) Pales lower as light approaches.
Memaw felt all kinds of birds
hovering near her

FRI., JULY 2, 10:07 PM
What did Impundulu want?

FRI., JULY 2, 10:10 PM
Wondered myself. She named
ancestors and gods I'd never
met—
limbs of Osiris in Brooks Brothers,
Isis in Fredrick's of Hollywood,
Jesus in torn polyester.

FRI., JULY 2, 10:12 PM
Ah, the birds wanted them then.

FRI., JULY 2, 10:17 PM
No. She said: *They waitin'* . . .
for you.
Then she died,
eyes wide,
fixed on me.

FRI., JULY 2, 10:28 PM
Dinn, dinn, dinn—
Dying's last words
mean nothing. What wants you
dead would have your head.

FRI., JULY 2, 10:29 PM
LOL! But I'm not dead, huh?

FRI., JULY 2, 11:21 PM
I'm not dead, right?

SAT., JULY 3, 3:00 AM
Anne? I'm not, right?

58 Who.

NARCISSUS TWEETS

@NarkeHunts
Followers 683
Following 1

@Artemis   Looked down into the silvered water and there he was.
The finest creature I've ever seen—the man I want to be. I'm in love.

@Eros   I want him inside me, but he only offers water. I've said: I'm
not parched, but I'm *parched*. He can't grasp nuance.

@Echo   Fuck off Fairy (fuck off fairy) repeat (repeat) after me (after
me): he'll kill you before you have me (he'll kill you . . . have me)

@GaiaNature   Turns out my water-spirit lover is a boy. Me too!
Guess I'm gay. At least I am in good company. Ask @Zeus about the
water bearer. #ganymedegame

@HeraCurses   That damned nymph @Echo rests near; my words
fall back to me. Why do I suffer her curse? #stalkerblues

@KaikiasBlows   Could you keep the wind still? Your kind kinks my
lover's skin, makes him turn from me.

@Odysseus   Do sirens sing in chorus? When he speaks, I speak. I can't hear him without hearing myself. It's getting old now.

@Poseidon   Did your trident strike this spring? The water's shallow, but get this: when I kiss my lover, I drown.

@Tethys   Everyone in your life moves. Do you chase after, or let them go? If what you thought was a pond is a puddle, do you mourn?

SEKHMET AFTER HOURS

Left of the sun disk on the dresser, I retire
the heirloom eye, place my ankh in a desert
diorama, a gift from some warrior's child. Hang
my lion's head on a gold-gilt wall mount, she casts
wild shadows on the ceiling—habit of insomnia.

When away from battlefields, simple deceits
pacify my full-blaze feral ego. Something vapid
to calm and divert attention from all those
warm rebels left alive. The fiercest
warriors know when to turn their backs.

I ignore fiction's mercies to wash
my real face, the one that knows of rivers
and smolder. Sure to splash water in both
eyes to smother the fires. Smoke replaces
iris and my blindness returns.

Standing straight before the vanity as if I can
see myself clearly. Here is where I'm hungry
skull, surging electric blue. Forced to raise
my unpainted face for a muddy flag and slake
my thirst with my own long, hard swallow.

A moment to consider the slow feast I've become
—offering famine and too much—to leeches
who have let my blood, including one
whose jawpinch I inherited. Such famished ghosts
can never be full, even after breaking fasts.

Each night a headlong stumble into glass that looks
just like me if I were not meant to rise before dawn.
Count the new shards in my hair, callouses under
brass rings; reminders of my hand to the miner's
ax and two sooty canaries left orphans to light.

The lion's head roars, side eyes my image
hoping not to face another of our undoings.

Shadows move, a mourner's bench.

62 Who.

PRIVILEGED GHOSTS OF PARIS

I.

Late again, running from Gare Montparnasse
when I intended Gare du Nord
past the Senegalese braiding shops, the women
waiting for their buses, a small boy tries to pry
his soccer ball from under a parked blue Fiat.
His dirty "Bafana, Bafana" jersey collects street
dust with each arm sweep beneath the car.

It's 8 am in Paris.

My Eurostar train leaves in 43 minutes
including the time it takes to cross the Seine
from Left Bank to Right.
Under is the only hope—the Metro.
On the opposite platform
a young girl stands in a beet-red dress,
ruching on the side.
I nudge my husband, pointing:

I saw her yesterday at Musée du Louvre—
same dress, same shoes.

Today, a rat is feeding on something
less fortunate avoiding the 3rd rail.
My train erupts from the eye
heading right.

II.

The seats are wider in the section
we've chosen. Unable to sit in an
adjoining seat, my husband adjusts
across the aisle from me, unfolds
the *Wall Street Journal*, settles.
The woman next to him is decidedly
French: full lips, hair swept
in loose chignon, and long legs.
He strikes up a conversation.

My companion, an older woman, short
hair, tweed jacket with velvet lapels,
body ambiguously rounded,

crosses her arms, looks me up and down:

what verb are you.

        You mean, what do I do?

She nods: *tell me small, purple.*

        Ma'am, I do necessary things.

She looks askance: *ma'am is for the living.*

My name's Gertie. You know me. Gertrude. Stein.

Her left hand presses buttons,

chair slowly reclines into

some traveler behind. Attendants

intercom: *Nous arriverons à Londres à 10 heures*

Gertie blurts: *a place is no new table, purple.*

        You don't know me like that! Don't call me purple.

She waves me away, unpolished nails: *oh phooey, blood red. blue blue.*

        mix. mix.

A BOX   *A PIECE of COFFEE*

        Bitch, what?

        Avant garde or abstruse?

        Genius comes easy when green

        wings spring from railway cars.

        Art knows struggle . . .

Our attendant offers Perrier.

I accept.

Gertie presses her button again, rises.

Upright, she looks out the window.

Every tree passes in a high-speed, cubist

blur. Our reflections make eye contact,

she places her hand over mine: *Rid a cover.*

Red weakens the hour, Hurt Color.

Here. Here.

We both are.

ANNE SEXTON CHECKS THE COMPOSER'S VITALS
(FROM THE ARCHIVED TRANSCRIPTS)

COMPOSER:

It's never been high—my pressure,

not me—I have. That's how we met.

Anyway, Arthur Rimbaud wrote a poem

I love, "Feasts of Hunger." In it a line, "Suck

the gaudy poison of the convolvuli."

If the convolvuli is what Sexton, the poet,

not you, the nurse, calls an infection,

then it's love. That's what it was those

countless times—there's something in me—

in my mouth—is it hunger?—that closes in

on the warmth of the other. Bites viscera collages

on organic walls. Tussles. Wallops. Heat-seeking

missiles can't unlaunch. What else is there to do

but dissolve into wondrous wails of feral praise?

Admire the broken seams of my own masterpiece,

my eternal opus. Hail Mary

full of something. And go on like nothing
isn't the most gracious lie.

SEXTON:

Pressure's normal.

PSYCHE ON PROZAC

The prescribed sleep makes her hear
everything clearly. Gone are nights
of grand departures and warring gods
vying for last words. This strange
season brings acute sighs of grubbed-out
thistle and ragworts resisting asphyxia.

She feels little about the vacancy
their slow death offers; rows
of poppy seeds and chickpeas
she might plant.

She feels little at all, actually.
Infernal torpor.

Hasn't even considered why
every mirror is veiled by gauze,
singed by the lantern's flame.
She has only the vaguest memory

of her former self or how that otter smooth
arrowscar on her arm got there or how
Venus thrust her head against the cellar floor.
She can't see the welted geometry
Worry's whipmarks left on her back.
Time, that immaculate housekeeper, long
since removed the yellow tape, mopped
blood pools and dusted crystal vessels
filled with black, rank water and gales.

All the Gods who saved her have new caseloads.
Her sisters have washed ashore.

Pleasure is crying, starved.
Tonight's supper is burning (again).
Psyche opens the oven door, places her bare
hands on the Calphalon pan spilling over
with ambrosia (again), tells the family
it's time to eat. They gather round her.
Cupid doesn't notice her blistering scalds,
or know she revels in being scorched awake,

in the moments before giving thanks

for their darkened portion

of forever.

There are limits to what

even Love can know.

SEKHMET'S QUERY

Though isn't it true, at some point,
assuming no air resistance, a stone
thrown upward with great velocity
will escape humble gravity?

REBEL FUGUE

it's possible to fall

in terrible love with burning

into jet bile currents

double meters, calinda bomba
body's gentle gestures to the
drummer

following the synchronous
thrums of trembling hands

swollen against stretched
membranes

seduced by godless sway

moments forgetting Lucifer, too,
was a beautiful musician

after all, there's no need to bring
cosmology into this

one's best hope to escape rhythmic
slipstreams is give way

flail limbs against walls

surrender to the notes in our pulse

exhaust both pain and pleasure

until, winded, we come up
for air

and should what swallowed us
not quite kill us,

exhume those rattling throatstones

balance on the fissured
ashen tongue

hail dawning, curse damning
through pursed lips

and live in violet

and breathe in mystery

Notes

The term *simulacra* derives from the Latin *simulare*, meaning "to make like" or simulate (*OED*, 1989, plural form: *simulacra*). According to Platonic understanding, the word raises issues of deception and illusion. However, the French philosopher and sociologist Jean Baudrillard rejected these previously held beliefs. Baudrillard asserted that the simulacrum did not hide the truth or forward false images. Rather, according to Baudrillard, the simulacrum was that which "hides the truth's nonexistence" (*Seduction*, 35), thereby making the simulacrum true. Jean Baudrillard, *Seduction* (New York: St. Martin's, 1990).

∞

Epigraph, p. vi: Albert Camus, *The Rebel: An Essay on Man in Revolt* (New York: Alfred A. Knopf, 1956).

∞

Epigraph, p. 2: Jean Baudrillard, *Simulacra and Simulation*, trans. Sheila Faria Glaser (Ann Arbor: University of Michigan Press, 1994).

∞

"Meeting Want" epigraph: Jean Baudrillard, *Simulacra and Simulation*, trans. Sheila Faria Glaser (Ann Arbor: University of Michigan Press, 1994).

∞

"Letter to My Would-Be Lover on Geometry and Ponds": Ouroboros is the serpent in Egyptian and Greek mythology depicted as eating its own tail, often symbolizing those things that appear to disappear.

∞

"Temptation of the Composer": Loosely based on the Sumerian myth of Inanna, the goddess of love, fertility, and warfare, before she makes her descent into the Underworld.

∞

"... And Repeating" epigraph: Jean Baudrillard, *Symbolic Exchange and Death* (London: Sage, 1993).

∞

"Sexton Texts a Dead Addict's Daughter during Polar Vortex": "Let us eat air, rock, coal, iron. Turn, my hungers" is borrowed from Arthur Rimbaud's poem "Fêtes de la faim" (Feasts of hunger). The poem, believed to have been written in 1872–73, is adapted from folk songs and addresses a broad range of topical themes. "Feasts of Hunger" was the source of the epigraph Anne Sexton used in her poem "Flee on Your Donkey," published in the *New Yorker*, May 7, 1966.

∞

"An Ingenue Texts Sexton before the Honey Moon": "feed, hungers, in the meadows of sounds!" is borrowed from Rimbaud's "Fêtes de la faim" (Feasts of hunger).

∞

"Sexton Texts a Backslider After Breaking Lent": The opening line "my hunger...my stomach makes me suffer" is attributable to Rimbaud's "Fêtes de la faim," and the line "Anne, Sister, flee on your donkey" is adapted from Rimbaud's original line "Anne, Anne, flee on your donkey," which Sexton used as the title of her poem.

∞

"Quiet Desperation Texts Sexton on Independence Day": See Sexton's "Flee on Your Donkey" for themes of chronic return to dysfunction.

∞

"The Lover Problem in Analogue (from Wittgenstein's *Lost Black Book*)": The *Lost Black Book* is a collection of imagined notes from Wittgenstein's lectures of 1933–35, which were published as *The Blue and Brown Books* (London: Blackwell, 1958). The first line of the poem, "If I give someone the order . . . string of *words*?" is reconfigured from a line on p. 3 of *The Blue Book*.

∞

"Dodecaphony" epigraph: Pierre-Simon LaPlace, *Essai philosophique sur les probabilités* (A philosophical essay on probabilities), 6th ed. (Paris: Bachelier, 1840).

∞

"Can?": See Wittgenstein, *Blue Book*, p. 15, for the relationship of the word *can* to logical possibility, thought, and meaning.

∞

"Who." epigraph: Jean Baudrillard, *De La Séduction* (Paris: Éditions Galilée, 1979).

∞

"Sexton Texts Tituba from a Bird Conservatory": See Rimbaud's "Fêtes de la faim" for the line "Eat, the stones a poor man breaks." The poem is dedicated to Margaret Walker, the first black woman to win the Yale Series of Younger Poets in 1942 with her collection *For My People*. One of the characters in Walker's book was Molly Means, a black sorceress. Tituba, a seventeenth-century West Indian slave, was the first accused in the Salem witch trials.

∞

"Privileged Ghosts of Paris": Certain italicized dialogue, relating to identity, attributed to Gertrude Stein, is language borrowed from the "Objects" section of *Tender Buttons*. Gertrude Stein, *Tender Buttons: Objects, Food, Rooms* (New York: Haskell House, 1970).

Acknowledgments

All thanks to the editors of the following publications, in which these poems—often in earlier versions—appeared:

American Poets: "Confessions from Here," "Sexton Texts Tituba from a Bird Conservatory" (alongside an introduction by D. A. Powell)

The Baffler: "Narcissus Tweets"

Best American Poetry 2015 and *KINFOLKS:* "If My Late Grandmother Were Gertrude Stein"

Callaloo: "Letters to My Would-Be Lover on Geometry and Ponds," "Meeting Want (Again)," "Letters to My Would-Be Lover on Dolls and Repeating"

Four Way Review: "Quiet Desperation Texts Sexton on Independence Day," "Sexton Texts a Dead Addict's Daughter during Polar Vortex"

Muzzle: "Prelude," "Hero(i)n"

Slab Literary Magazine: "The Dentist's Wife," "The Mine Owner's Wife"

I send thanks to the institutions that have offered fellowships and space to think through this work—The Bread Loaf Writers' Conference, Callaloo, Cave Canem, the Kresge Arts Foundation, and the University of Michigan Helen Zell Writers' Program.

I owe a debt of gratitude to my friends and teachers who helped me along the path—Chris Abani, Toi Dericotte, Linda Gregerson, A. Van Jordan, Laura Kasischke, Gregory Pardlo, D. A. Powell, Khadijah Queen, Lyrae Van-Clief Stefanon, and Keith Taylor. And so much love and thanks to every reader in every workshop who has ever offered feedback, especially my 2013 MFA cohort. I thank every poet who writes the good and hard work—your words reach out to others even when you don't know it.

Thank you to the "ride or die" family I was born to—Mommy and Rae. And the family I met along the way—Haya Alfarhan, the Atkins, Black Excellence, the late David Blair, Gillian and Matthew Eaton, Aricka Foreman, Ernesto Mercer, and the artistic community of Detroit.

A shiny thank-you for my "blud" sisterhood's undying love and confidence—Nora Chassler, Tarfia Faizullah, Vievee Francis, Rachel McKibbens, Gala Mukomolova, and Ladan Osman. You are goddesses of the highest order.

Obrigada to my familial ancestors, known and unknown, and my many literary ancestors, including Margaret Walker, Anne Sexton, and Gertrude Stein.

A special thank-you to Carl Phillips for his brilliance, direction, vision, and belief in this book.

And, above all, the boldest, brightest and deepest thanks to my husband, Emery, and our double helixes—Trey, Wes, Eli, and Willow—for teaching me what love is and does.